DISCOVER AND DO!

LIGHT

Written by Jane Lacey

Enslow PUBLISHING

Published in 2023 by Enslow Publishing, LLC
29 East 21st Street, New York, NY 10010

Editor: Katie Dicker
Designer: Clare Nicholas
Series Designer: Rocket Design (East Anglia) Ltd

Manufactured in the United States of America

CPSIA compliance information: Batch #CSENS23: For further information contact
Enslow Publishing LLC, New York, New York at 1-800-398-2504.

Please visit our website, www.enslowpublishing.com. For a free color catalog of all our high-quality books,
call toll free 1-800-398-2504 or fax 1-877-980-4454.

Cataloging-in-Publication Data

Names: Lacey, Jane.

Title: Light / Jane Lacey.

Description: New York : Enslow Publishing, 2023. | Series: Discover and do! | Includes glossary and index.

Identifiers: ISBN 9781978530669 (pbk.) | ISBN 9781978530683 (library bound) | ISBN 9781978530676 (6pack) | ISBN 9781978530690 (ebook)

Subjects: LCSH: Light--Juvenile literature. | Color--Juvenile literature.

Classification: LCC QC360.L334 2023 | DDC 535--dc23

Picture credits:

t=top b=bottom m=middle l=left r=right

Shutterstock: La Gorda cover/title page l, MaryDesy cover/title page r, 4, 10b and 31b, Anatolir 5tl and 7tr, Ara Hovhannisyan 5br and 8m, Diki Prayogo 6t, Maurice Tricatelle 8b, Sonya illustration 12, Blablo101 14tr and 29tr, vectorpouch 14m, Lina Truman 15tr, OnD 15tr, baldezh 16b, GoodStudio 16br, equinoxvect 18b, Bukavik 18br, Kateryna Lomakina 20tr, Maha Heang 245789 20b, Flat vectors 23tr and 30b, diluck 24l and 31m, Ebichan 24br, Phovoir 25tr, Oceloti 26tr and 28, Ann in the uk 26b; Getty: anuwat meereewee 5tr, 18tl and 30t, vectortatu 6b, Kerkez 7m, FORGEM 7b, Xurzon 10tl and 32, Macrovector 14b and 29br, kertlis 16tr, OGI75 19tr, Bigmouse108 20br, hekakoskinen 20bl, zvukmedia 22tr, artcyclone 22b, Anastasiia_M 27tr and 31t.

All design elements from Shutterstock.

Craft models from a previous series by Q2AMedia.

DISCOVER AND DO!

LIGHT

Written by Jane Lacey

Enslow PUBLISHING

CONTENTS

Words that appear in **bold** can be found in the glossary on pages 28–29.

WHAT IS LIGHT?

Light is a kind of energy. The sun is the greatest source of natural light on Earth. Our eyes need light to see, so when the sun goes down at night, we turn on lights or burn candles to see.

At night, we use **artificial** light to help us to see.

Travelling light

Light travels in a straight line at 186,000 miles (300,000 km) per second. It is the fastest moving thing in the universe! Light from the sun takes about 8 minutes and 20 seconds to travel through space to Earth. You must never look directly at the sun. It is too bright for our eyes.

Luminous

Things that give out light are **luminous**. Some luminous things give out brighter, more intense light than others. The brightness of car headlights is more intense than the brightness of candlelight, for example.

This flashlight is luminous. It gives out a beam of light to read by.

Moonlight is pale because it is reflected light from the sun.

Reflected light

We see some objects when light bounces off them, or is reflected into our eyes. The moon is not luminous so it does not give out light. We see the moon when the sun shines on it. The moon reflects sunlight into our eyes.

WHAT IS DARK?

Where there is no light, it is dark. It is dark wherever light cannot reach–in your bedroom when you turn out the light and close the curtains, or at the bottom of the sea and in deep caves, for example.

Day and night

Earth takes 24 hours to spin around once in space. It is night when the half of Earth you are on is turning away from the sun. It is day when your half of Earth is facing the sun.

Earth turns every 24 hours. It is day for the half facing the sun and night for the half facing away from the sun.

Living in the dark

Some animals, such as owls, have large eyes to help them see in the dark. Other animals use their senses of smell and touch in the darkness. Some deep-sea fish and night insects make their own light and glow in the dark to attract prey or find a mate.

Glowworms give off a green glow or a flashing light to attract a mate in the dark.

ACTIVITY

MAKE A MODEL EARTH

Ask an adult to help you with this activity.

You will need:

- **bowl and spoon**
- **water**
- **flour**
- **salt**
- **round balloon**
- **newspaper**
- **straight stick about 20 inches (50 cm) long**
- **pen and paints**
- **atlas**
- **flashlight**

1. In a bowl, stir 12 fluid ounces (375 ml) of water, 1/3 cup (75 g) of flour, and 1.5 teaspoons (7 g) of salt together to make a smooth paste like glue.

2. Blow up the balloon and tie the end securely. Tear strips of newspaper about 2.6 inches x 1 inch (6 cm x 3 cm) and dip them into the paste.

3. Stick the strips onto the balloon in layers to make a round ball-shaped "Earth." Leave to dry. When the paper is dry, ask an adult to help you pop the balloon and push the stick carefully through the center of the ball and out the other side.

4. Paint the ball to look like Earth, with the stick going through the North and South Pole. Use an atlas to find where you are on Earth and mark this position on your planet.

5. In a darkened room, hold your model Earth in the beam of your flashlight. Gradually turn the stick and watch your part of Earth move from day to night.

LIGHT RAYS

Light travels away from a light source in straight lines called rays. Sometimes you can see rays of light from the sun shining through trees, from behind clouds, or through a window.

Rays of sunlight are shining through gaps between the trees in this forest.

Lighting up the dark

Rays from a strong light source, such as the sun, travel long distances and light up a large area. Rays from a weaker source, such as a candle, travel shorter distances and light up a small area.

One direction

Light can only travel in straight lines (or beams). You can clearly see the straight, narrow beam of a flashlight or car headlight in the dark, for example. A theater spotlight sends out a beam of light to show a dancer on the stage, leaving the rest of the theater in darkness.

A lighthouse sweeps a beam of light across the water at night to warn ships of dangerous rocks.

ACTIVITY

HIT THE TARGET!

Ask an adult to help you with this activity.

You will need:

- **1 square of paper and 5 squares of strong card stock 6 inches x 6 inches (15 cm x 15 cm)**
- **scissors**
- **pencil and paints (or colored pens)**
- **modeling clay**
- **ruler**
- **flashlight**

1. Fold the paper in half both ways to find the center point. Open it out and put it on top of four of the card stock squares.

2. Ask an adult to push sharp scissors through the center of the four pieces of card stock, using the paper as a guide. Cut a small circle around each hole. Leave the fifth square of card stock uncut–this will be your target. Draw a target around the center.

3. Push each piece of card stock into a ball of modeling clay (for a stand). Line them up on a table or on the floor about 8 inches (20 cm) apart, with the target at one end of the line. Shine the flashlight beam through the hole at the other end of the line. Can you line up the holes so the beam of light shines through them and hits the target?

SHADOWS

Light cannot go around corners. When something solid gets in the way of light rays, light cannot shine through it or go around it. This creates a shadow that is shaped like the solid object.

Different shadows

As Earth turns around, the sun seems to move across the sky. In the morning and evening, when the sun is low in the sky, your shadow is longer than you are. At midday, when the sun is overhead, your shadow is shorter.

MAKE A SUNDIAL

Ask an adult to help you with this activity.

You will need:

- **strong, thick card stock**
- **length of dowel (thin rod of wood), about 10 inches (25 cm) long**
- **tape or glue**
- **compass**
- **ruler**
- **waterproof marker**
- **waterproof paints**

1. Ask an adult to make a hole in the card stock half-way down one of the long sides, about 1 inch (2.5 cm) from the edge.

2. Push the dowel into the hole so the base of the dowel is level with the underside of the card stock. Tape or glue it in place so it stands upright. Alternatively, place the sundial on some grass and push the dowel through the hole into the grass to secure it.

3. Use a compass to place the sundial so the stick edge of the card is facing south.

4. On a sunny day, on every hour, with your ruler and marker draw a line along the shadow made by the stick. Write the time on each line: 9:00, 10:00, 11:00, etc., and paint each segment.

5. Put your sundial in the same place to tell the time on sunny days. The shadow will move throughout the day as the position of the sun changes.

SHINING THROUGH

Light can shine through transparent materials. Glass, clear plastic, and clean water are transparent–you can see through them. Light cannot shine through opaque materials such as wood, metal and card.

Translucent

Some materials are **translucent**, which means some light can pass through them. Sunglasses are translucent. They help to protect your eyes from harmful sun rays. Tracing paper and tissue paper are both translucent materials. When you look through them you can see some light, but only blurred shapes.

Materials

Materials are often chosen because of the way light shines through them. Glass, for example, is transparent. Glass windows let you see in and out. Thick bedroom curtains are opaque. They keep out the light to help you sleep.

You can clearly see how much water is in a glass beaker (left). Plastic beakers let less light through them.

ACTIVITY

MAKE A LIGHT AND SHADOWS COLLAGE

You will need:

- **selection of paper (e.g. white paper, colored tissue paper, tracing paper)**
- **foil**
- **thin card stock**
- **thin white cotton material**
- **scissors**
- **sheet of clear plastic**
- **glue**
- **powerful flashlight**

1. Cut different shapes from the paper, foil, card, and cotton. Stick them onto one side of the clear plastic sheet to make a picture.

2. Try to guess which materials will let light through. Make a chart to show your guesses.

3. In a dark room, shine the flashlight through the plastic sheet onto a white wall. How good were your guesses? What do you notice about the shadows?

REFLECTION

When rays of light hit something, they bounce off it, like a ball bouncing off a hard surface. This is called reflection. Different surfaces cause the light rays to reflect in different ways.

The reflection in this water becomes blurred when light bounces off the ripples in different directions.

Smooth and rough

When light hits a smooth surface, such as flat water in a pond, it bounces off in one direction and you see a reflection. Light bounces off rough, uneven surfaces in all directions. You don't see a clear reflection in a choppy sea, for example.

Mirrors

Mirrors are made of smooth glass covering a layer of shiny metal. When light rays hit the mirror, they bounce straight back and you see your reflection.

You can see your reflection in a flat, shiny mirror.

ACTIVITY

MAKE A KALEIDOSCOPE

You will need:

- **3 rectangles of shiny card stock, all the same size, about 8 inches x 2 inches (20 cm x 5 cm) or very shiny foil glued onto card**
- **tape**
- **pencil**
- **white paper**
- **scissors**
- **colored paper shapes or metallic confetti**
- **plastic food wrap**

1. Tape the foil card rectangles together to make a triangular **prism** with the shiny side facing inwards.

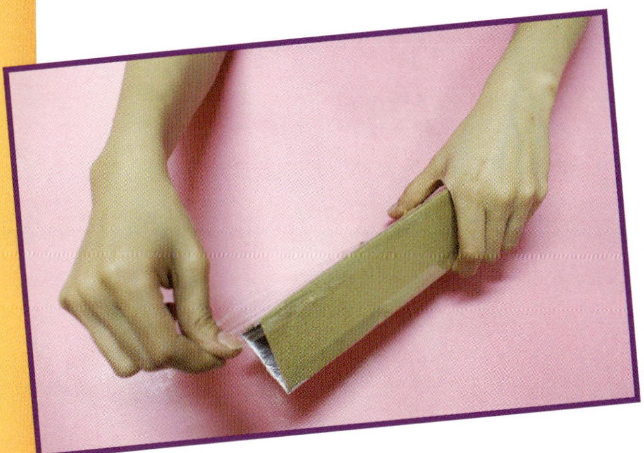

2. Trace around the triangular end on the white paper and cut out the triangle shape. Stick the paper triangle to one end of the prism.

Drop the colored paper shapes (or confetti) into the prism and seal the open end of your kaleidoscope with plastic food wrap.

3. Hold your kaleidoscope up to the light and look through the plastic wrap. You will see a repeated pattern of colored shapes. Shake the kaleidoscope to change the pattern.

Light from the colored shapes bounces from mirror to mirror and you see several reflections that make repeated patterns.

REFRACTION

Light travels through water and glass more slowly than it travels through air. When light passes from glass or water to the surrounding air, the rays slightly change direction and bend. This is called refraction.

This pencil seems to bend because light rays from the pencil change direction as they leave the water.

Bending light

Refraction makes straight objects, such as a pencil or a canoe paddle, look bent when they are half in and half out of water. This is because light changes direction as it moves from water to air.

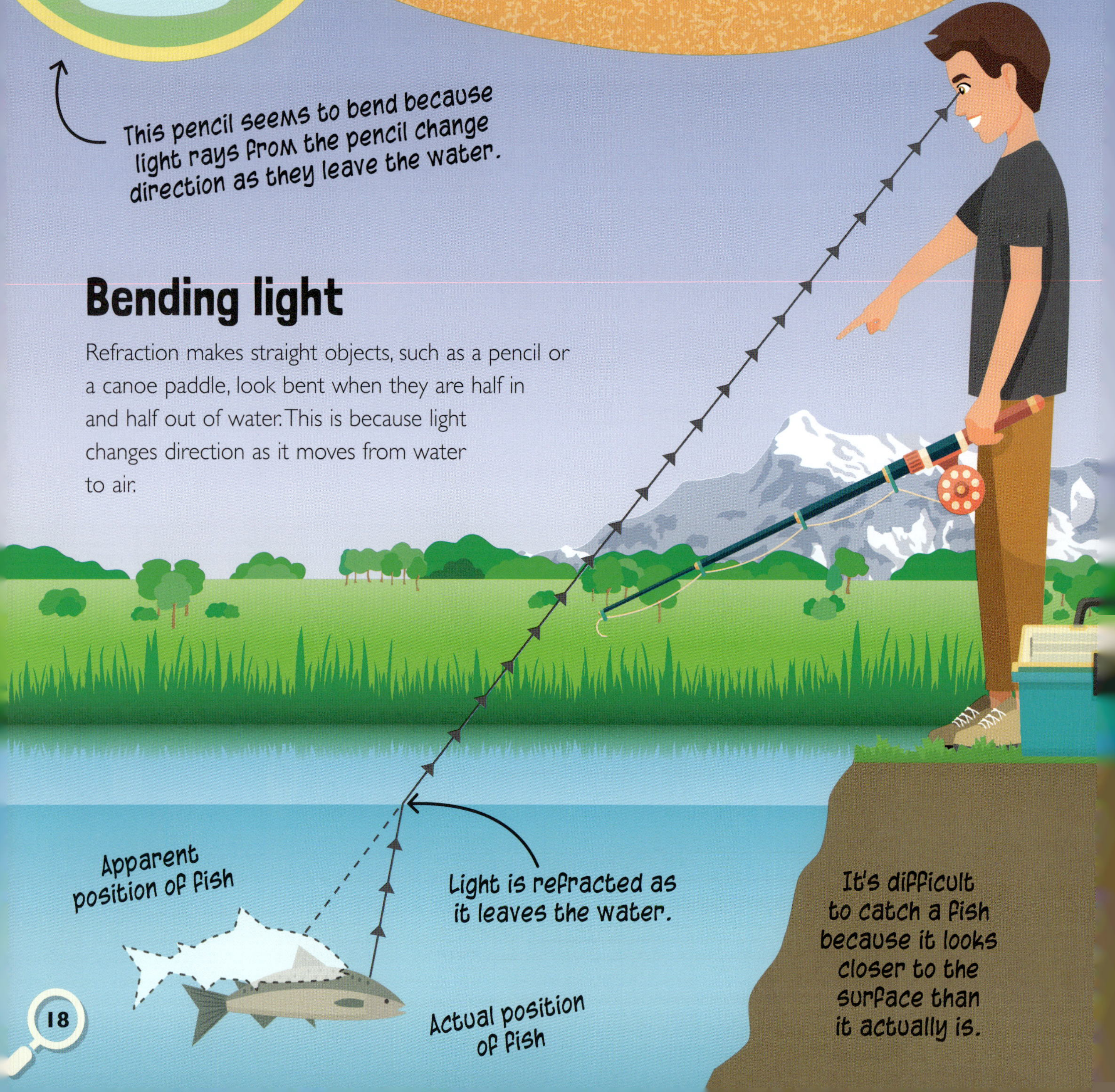

Bending shapes

If you look through a big raindrop on a windowpane, the objects you see through the glass will appear to have strange shapes. This is because rays of light bend as they travel through the glass and the water, and change the shape of the things you see.

You see distorted shapes through the raindrops on a window because the light rays are refracted.

ACTIVITY

USE REFRACTION FOR A MAGIC TRICK!

You will need:

- **bowl**
- **coin**
- **modeling clay**
- **jug of water**

1. Place the bowl on a table. Attach a coin to the bottom near side of the bowl with modeling clay.

2. Ask a friend to look at the coin and then move slowly backwards and stop when the coin disappears from view.

3. Pour some water into the bowl. Your friend will be amazed to see the coin reappear!

Light reflected from the coin is bent as it leaves the water and goes into the air, helping your friend to see the coin again.

BIGGER AND SMALLER

Lenses are pieces of curved glass or other transparent material, such as plastic. They refract light rays shining through them and cause them to change direction.

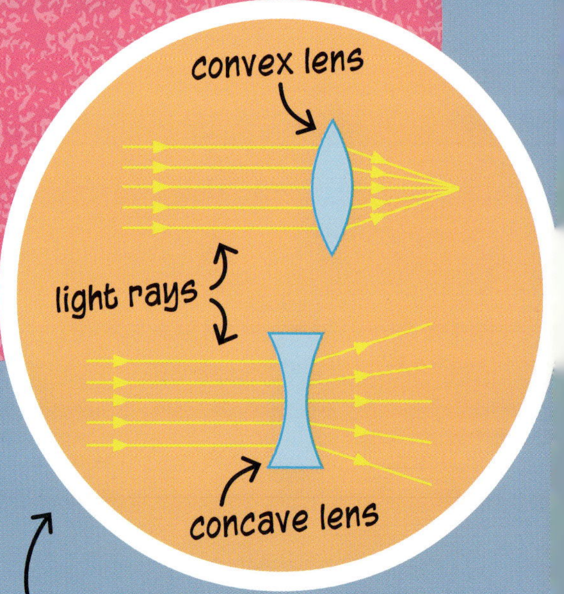

Convex lenses refract light rays inwards and concave lenses refract light rays outwards.

Concave and convex

Lenses in glasses help to focus images onto the back of our eyes (see page 25). **Convex lenses** help people who cannot see near things clearly. **Concave lenses** help people who cannot see distant things well.

Microscope

A **microscope** uses convex lenses to make tiny things look thousands of times bigger than they really are. Light is reflected off a mirror onto the **sample** and through a series of lenses to reach our eyes.

We use a microscope to look at tiny objects such as plant cells (left).

MAKE A MICROSCOPE

Ask an adult to help you with this activity.

You will need:
- **clear plastic bottle**
- **scissors**
- **small mirror**
- **modeling clay**
- **cup of water**
- **human hair**

1. Ask an adult to help you cut the top off the bottle. Then cut two narrow vertical strips out of opposite sides of the bottle, and two short horizontal slits near the top of the bottle in the other two sides (see the template below).

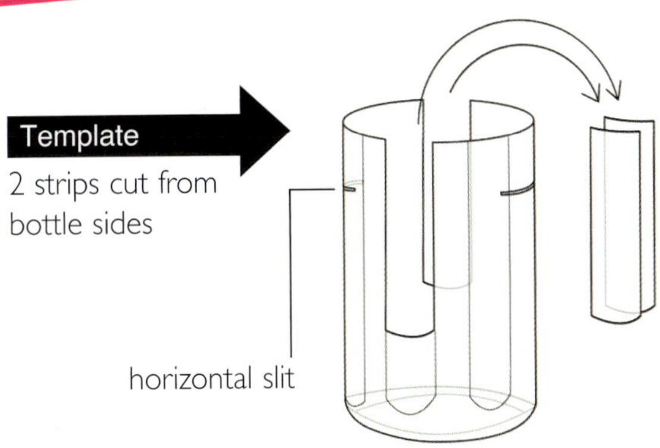

2. Angle the small mirror in the bottom of the bottle to reflect light upwards. Use the modeling clay as a support. Push each end of one of the vertical strips into the small horizontal slits to make a platform.

3. Drip one drop of water onto the platform to form a convex lens. Use the other strip as a slide. Put a hair onto the strip and hold it under the platform. The hair will be magnified by the water drop.

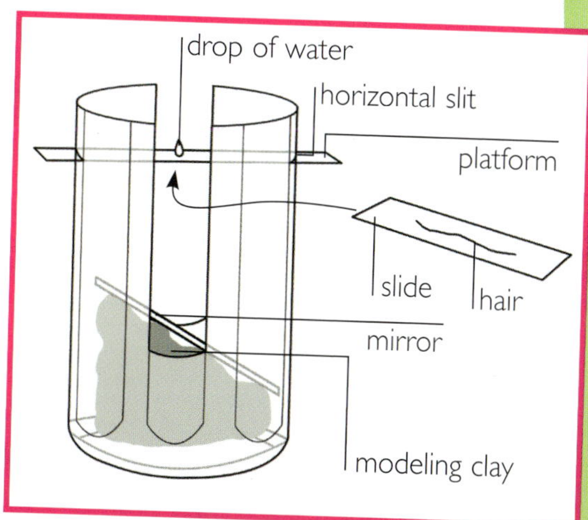

You can use a **magnifying glass** to make it look even bigger!

DIFFERENT KINDS OF LIGHT

Luminous objects glow in different ways. **Incandescent light** is given off by heat. The sun gives off incandescent light. When **electricity** passes through older light bulbs, the wire becomes red hot and glows with incandescent light.

Light in nature

Lightning is a type of natural incandescent light that you see in a storm. During a storm, natural electricity builds up in a cloud and creates a huge spark that we see as a flash of lightning and hear as a crash of thunder.

Fluorescence

Things that are **fluorescent** do not glow by themselves. They glow in the dark, for example, when light shines on them. Fluorescent strips on clothes glow in the dark when they are caught in the headlights of a car or truck.

Fluorescent strips help to keep you visible and safe when walking at night.

ACTIVITY

MAKE A GLOW-IN-THE-DARK MOBILE

Ask an adult to help you with this activity.

You will need:

- **colored fluorescent card stock**
- **pencil**
- **scissors**
- **glue**
- **hole puncher**
- **string**
- **coat hanger**
- **flashlight**

1. Fold the card stock in half and draw on nighttime shapes such as ghosts, stars, moons, and owls. Cut the shapes out of the doubled card stock.

2. Stick the shapes together so both sides are fluorescent. Punch a hole near the top of each shape and attach different lengths of string.

3. Tie your nighttime shapes onto the coat hanger and hang it in your bedroom.

4. Test how your mobile glows best: in a completely dark room, in flashlight light or in daylight.

SEEING AND LIGHT

We see things around us when light reflects off them into our eyes. It's difficult to see at night when there is only a little light. We see nothing at all in total darkness.

Letting in light

The black circle in the middle of our eyes, called the **pupil**, is a hole that lets in light. The **iris** controls how much light enters our eyes by making the pupil bigger or smaller. This helps our eyes to cope with different strengths of light.

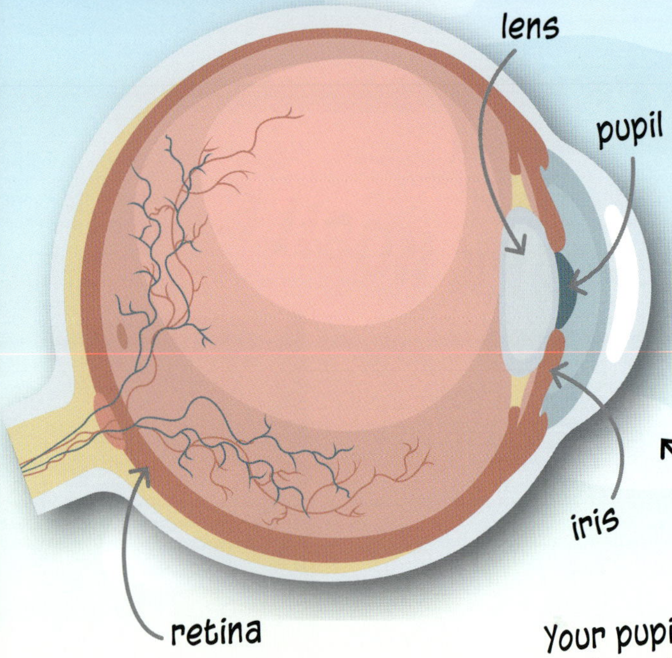

This diagram shows some of the different parts of our eyes.

Lenses

Inside our eyes, behind the pupil, is a lens. Reflected light from an object, such as a flower, shines through the pupil onto the lens. The lens focuses this light onto the **retina** and makes an upside-down image of the flower. Our brain turns the image around so we see the flower the right way up.

Light is reflected from this flower into our eyes. The magnifying glass is a lens that makes the flower look bigger.

ACTIVITY

MAKE A CAMERA

Ask an adult to help you with this activity.

You will need:

- **small square box without a lid (such as a gift box)**
- **tracing paper**
- **stape**
- **lamp**
- **magnifying glass**

1. Stretch the tracing paper tightly over the open end of the box and tape it in place to make a smooth screen.

2. Ask an adult to make a pinhole in the middle of the opposite side of the box. In a darkened room, point the pinhole at a bright object such as a lamp.

3. Hold the magnifying glass to act as a lens between the lamp and the pinhole. You will see the lamp reflected upside down onto the screen.

Your camera shows how our eyes work. Light enters the small hole (pupil) and shines onto the tracing paper (retina).

COLORED LIGHT

Light around us seems to be white but, in fact, it is made up of different colors. We only see these colors when light is refracted through something transparent, such as a glass prism.

A glass prism splits white light into the colors of the rainbow.

The spectrum

The colors that make up light are called the **spectrum**. When light shines through a glass prism, the colors travel at different speeds and bend a slightly different amount. The colors separate and we see red, orange, yellow, green, light blue, dark blue, and purple.

Seeing colors

Our eyes see red, blue, and green light. We see the colors of a rainbow when these three colors mix and blend together. A filter is a piece of colored translucent material, such as glass or tissue paper. A filter only lets light of the same color through.

We see the different colors of these balloons when mixtures of red, blue, and green light are reflected from them.

ACTIVITY

MIX THE COLORS OF LIGHT

You will need:

- **rectangles of card stock 25 inches x 8 inches (63 cm x 20 cm) to make 3 long tubes**
- **tape**
- **3 flashlights**
- **red, blue, and green tissue paper**
- **large sheet of white paper**

1. Roll each piece of card stock lengthwise to make tubes that will fit snugly around the ends of the flashlights. Tape the long edges together.

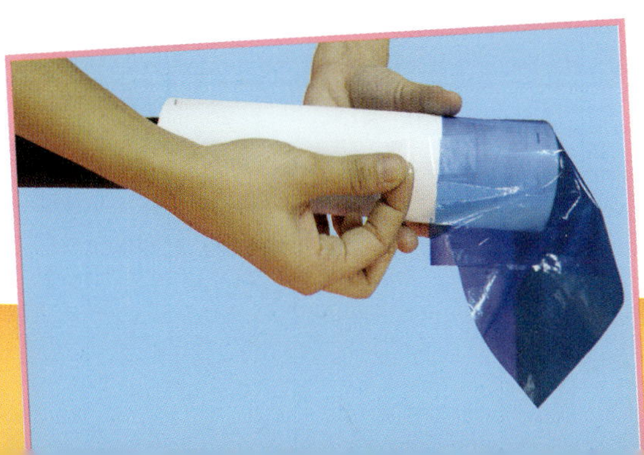

2. Tape a tube to the end of each flashlight and tape a piece of colored tissue paper over the end of each tube.

3. In a dark room, shine the flashlights onto the white paper and experiment by mixing the three colors of light.

What different colors can you make?

Glossary

artificial
When something is artificial it is human-made rather than natural.

concave lenses
Concave lenses are curved inwards in the middle. They refract light rays outwards.

convex lenses
Convex lenses are curved outwards in the middle. They refract light rays inwards.

electricity
Electricity is a type of energy. We use it to power lights and machines.

energy
Energy is the power that makes things work.

fluorescent
Things that are fluorescent glow in the dark when light shines on them.

incandescent light
Hot objects give off incandescent light. The light from a fire is incandescent.

iris
Your iris is the part of your eye that makes your pupil bigger or smaller to let more or less light through.

lens
A lens is a curved piece of glass or other transparent material that causes light rays to change direction.

luminous
Things that give out light are luminous. The sun, a flashlight, and a candle are all luminous.

magnifying glass
A magnifying glass is a lens used to make objects look bigger.

materials
Materials are what things are made of. For example, a book is made of paper and a sweater is made of wool.

microscope
A microscope is a piece of equipment that uses lenses to make tiny objects look bigger.

opaque

You cannot see through things that are opaque and light cannot shine through them.

prism

A prism is a solid shape with three flat sides.

pupil

Your pupil is the black circle in the center of your eye. It is the opening that lets light into your eye.

ray

A ray is a narrow beam of light.

reflected

When light is reflected, it bounces off a surface.

refraction

Refraction is the slight bend in light rays when they pass between air and other transparent materials.

retina

The retina is at the back of your eye. It receives images from the lens and sends them to your brain.

sample

A sample is a small part of something used in a test. A sample of hair can be looked at under a microscope, for example.

shadow

A shadow is a dark shape caused by something coming between rays of light and a surface.

spectrum

The spectrum is all the colors of light. We see the spectrum when sunlight shines through raindrops and a rainbow appears in the sky.

translucent

Translucent materials only let some light shine through them. We cannot see clearly through translucent materials.

transparent

Light shines through transparent materials such as glass. We can see through them clearly.

Quiz

1. **At what speed does light travel?**
   a) 186 miles/sec
   b) 1,860 miles/sec
   c) 18,600 miles/sec
   d) 186,000 miles/sec

2. **How does light travel?**
   a) in straight lines
   b) in curved lines
   c) in zigzag lines
   d) in wavy lines

3. **When the sun is low:**
   a) your shadow is short
   b) your shadow is long
   c) your shadow is wide
   d) your shadow is thin

4. **Which materials DON'T let light through?**
   a) transparent materials
   b) translucent materials
   c) opaque materials
   d) soft materials

5. **Which of the following is true?**
   a) light travels quickest through air
   b) light travels quickest through water
   c) light travels quickest through glass
   d) light travels the same through all materials

6. **Convex lenses refract light:**
   a) outwards
   b) inwards
   c) upwards
   d) downwards

7. **Lightning is a type of:**
   a) reflected light
   b) refracted light
   c) fluorescent light
   d) incandescent light

8. **How do fluorescent materials glow?**
   a) by themselves
   b) when they get hot
   c) when light shines on them
   d) when electricity powers them

9 **Which is NOT a part of the eye?**

a) pupil
b) iris
c) lily
d) retina

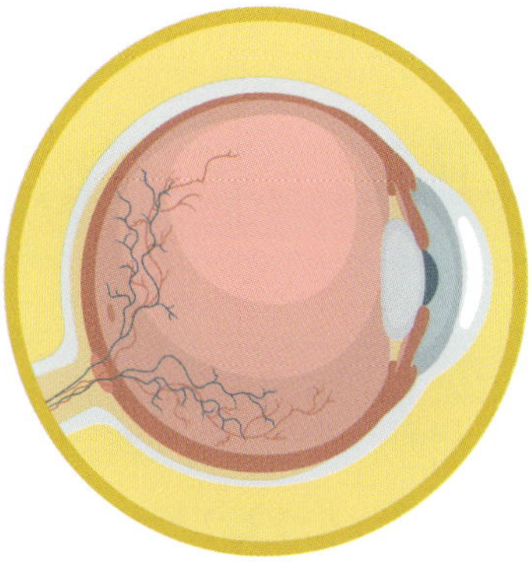

10 **Our eyes see:**

a) red, blue, and yellow light
b) red, blue, and green light
c) red, green, and yellow light
d) blue, green, and yellow light

ANSWERS 1d, 2a, 3b, 4c, 5a, 6b, 7d, 8c, 9c, 10b

FURTHER INFORMATION

BOOKS

A Question of Science: Why does a mirror show things back to front? by Anna Claybourne, Wayland

Be a Scientist: Investigating Light by Jacqui Bailey, Wayland

Boom Science: Light by Georgia Amson-Bradshaw, Franklin Watts

Extreme Science: Spectacular Light and Sound by Jon Richards, Wayland

WEBSITES

All about light: www.bbc.co.uk/bitesize/topics/zbssgk7/articles/z2s4xfr

Further light experiments to try: www.fizzicseducation.com.au/category/150-science-experiments/light-sound-experiments

Find out more and test yourself: www.dkfindout.com/uk/science/light

Index